The Only Prospecting Guide
You'll Ever Need!

The Only Prospecting Guide You'll Ever Need!

An Easy-To-Learn, Simple-To-Apply, No-Fail Prospecting System For Any IBO Who Has Ever Asked Themselves The Question,

"Who Do I Talk To Next Now That My Original List of Names Has Run Out?"

Bob Burg

Executive Books

The Only Prospecting Guide You'll Ever Need!

Copyright © 2000 - Bob Burg
Published by Executive Books
Mechanicsburg, Pennsylvania

EXECUTIVE BOOKS
206 West Allen Street
Mechanicsburg, PA 17055
800-233-2665
www.executivebooks.com

Printed in the United States of America

ISBN: 0-937539-50-3

Table of Contents

Preface

Okay, there's good news and bad news. Which one would you like first?

Let's begin with the good news. You truly have your hands on the best business opportunity on the face of the Earth. You are in the exact right place to build your business, and at the exact right time. Your line of mentorship is the best in the business, the business-building *system* you get to learn from is tops, and the corporation behind your business is beyond reproach, with years of experience and success. In fact, they have created millionaires and have been a vehicle for financial and time freedom for free-enterprising individuals just like you for over 40 years.

And now, they have even taken advantage of the latest technological trends and equipment, invested millions upon millions of dollars in this technology, hooked up with other top industry leaders, and provided for you an infrastructure that truly puts you in the driver's seat on the highway of life. The "information highway" you might say. In fact, you've got your hands on - as my friend Burke Hedges says - DreamBiz.com!

That's the good news. And you'll agree, it's pretty darn good!!

So, what's the bad news?

Well, actually, it's not really even bad news. More like, "real-world" news. And that is simply the following: even though you are an Independent Business Owner affiliated with the greatest high-tech company on the planet, with potential to make a tremendous sum of money and enjoy a lifestyle of comfort and freedom... THIS IS A PEOPLE BUSINESS!!!!! It always has been, is now, and always will be.

So, Bob, it's a people business. Big deal. Why is that bad news? Oh, I'm sorry; I mean, "real-world" news? What I mean is, why are

1

you making a big deal about the fact that it's a people business? Of course it is.

Allow me to explain. People can be difficult. There. . . I said it. And, quite frankly, it's no big surprise to you. They are not like you and me. Presented with a chance to break out of mediocrity, reclaim their lives, provide better for their family, give more back to the planet, and live a life of freedom as embodied by the American Dream, most people will just say no. Now, I believe in the saying, "Just say no" when it comes to certain things, which I'm sure you can imagine. But why would anyone "just say no" to this business?

Want to know the answer? Okay, here it is. . . "I don't know."

On the other hand, more good news. It doesn't really matter. That's because there are enough people out there who are looking for this exact opportunity, that all you have to do is go through enough of the "no's" that eventually you'll find the yesses. And it doesn't matter how many say no. It doesn't matter because:

You know there's an endless number of people out there you can confidently approach with ease in a way that you won't have to feel nervous or uptight, and they'll be totally open to the idea of being approached by you regarding a business opportunity.

Ahh, Bob, now I understand the "bad news" part. I don't really feel the way you just described me in the previous paragraph.

I understand how you feel. Actually, many people have felt the same way. What they found, however, was that there was a prospecting method they could use that would forever allow them to put as many people in front of the plan as they so desired. And in doing so, they never, ever again had to ask themselves the question:

2

"Who do I talk to next, now that my original list of names has run out?"

The information in this booklet will take you on a short, real-world, step-by-step, and profitable trip to putting in front of you a never ending list of new, quality prospects. You will find this information similar to a map that will lead you to buried treasure; the treasure being qualified and quality names, names, names, names, and more names.

Before we move on to chapter one, I must make two statements.

#1 This method absolutely and unquestionably works, and has been used with great results by many of your fellow IBOs. Luck has nothing to do with anything; it is strictly a matter of cause and effect. Do the right things, and you'll get the right results (This, of course, takes nothing away from G-d's hand in the process - it is how He designed His world).

#2 If it seems like I'm bragging, I'm not. I take absolutely no credit for these methods, techniques, success principles, etc. I've learned more from your leaders than I've ever taught. In fact, I can genuinely say, "I haven't had an original thought in my life!" However, if there's one thing that possibly I've been good at, it is learning from others, applying other people's methods successfully, and then, as a gift from G-d, being able to successfully teach others how to do the same thing.

I wish you the best of success as you help lots of people change their lives.

GO DIAMOND!

Bob Burg

Chapter 1
The Mindset
(Your Only Inventory Is People)

You began with a healthy list of names. People you knew. Family, friends, lots of acquaintances. And since you were so totally fired up and excited about this incredible opportunity, you knew (and you knew that you knew) that all those people on your initial names list would be just as excited about it as you were. . . **NOT!**

You made some calls and got some no's. Handed out some really cool, high-tech-type disks and got some more no's. Approached others verbally and got some more no's. Went back to calling on the phone and received even *more* no's. It may have even begun to remind you of that hit song from the early 70s that went something like, "No no no, no no nononono, no nono, nono no no, nono no no . . ."

Uh-oh. What a lousy feeling. What's going on? Why aren't these people interested? Are they crazy? What is it they're not interested in: financial freedom, more money, a less-stressful lifestyle?

Let's back up just a bit, to the very first words uttered in the previous paragraph. They were, "Uh-oh."

Uh-oh, meaning, "Uh-oh, if many more people continue to tell me 'no' I'm going to sooner or later (most likely sooner) run out of names of people to call. Then what will I do? I'll be out of business!"

Now, we know how important it is to keep exposing the business to people, right? After all, the Diamonds always teach, "He or she who shows the most plans, wins." In other words, it doesn't really matter how many people say "no" as long as you find enough people who say "yes."

Secret of the Diamonds

At the time of this writing, I've been privileged to have spoken at over 60 major Diamond Functions. I remember when I began speaking to various organizations and I'd ask the Diamonds, "What is it that has made you so successful in the business?" They'd talk about the system of books, tapes, seminars, functions, voice mail, the Eight-Step Pattern, etc. Then I'd ask, "Well, a lot of IBO's follow that, and with great success. I mean, many of them are obviously on the fast track to Diamond, but they're not there yet, so what is the *determining factor*. . . the reason why you are Diamond while they are not?"

Their answer was always - now get this - always the same: "We Diamonds have simply shown the plan to more people than those who are not yet Diamonds."

Could that really be it? But that's so simple.

Ah, yes *Grasshopper* (remember the old Kung Fu television show?), *simple,* but not necessarily *easy.*

You might be asking yourself, "But how do I find all those people to talk to? Because the way things are going right now, my list of names is running out fast and furious. And the more I try to talk to new people I meet about this incredible business that I'm so excited about, the more they seem to be staying away from me, and even avoiding me. . . in droves!"

How to find all those new people to talk to? That's exactly what we're going to address.

By the way, about those people telling you "no?" That was bad enough, but wasn't the worst part the fact that you could sense you were beginning to sound needy, if not downright desperate? As though you needed them more than they needed you? Actually, you would even have settled for someone just to affirm you were doing

6

the right thing. But people are interesting, aren't they? If they sense desperation, they are less inclined to be interested. And that was definitely happening.

Posture

That's where a concept called "posture" comes in. I define posture as coming across to your prospect as though you care. . . but not *that* much! What's interesting about posture is that the more of it you have, the more people are responsive to you in a positive manner. When they sense you don't care that much whether they are interested, they suddenly become more interested. *"Hmm, what is he doing that's so good that he doesn't really care that I'm not interested?"* And even if they're not interested, it gives you more confidence as you move on to your next prospect.

There are only two ways to have *true* posture. "True" posture, by the way is just a bit different from regular posture. Regular posture is *coming across* to your prospect as though you don't care that much. True Posture is when you *truly* don't care that much! Please don't get me wrong. Yes, you care about the person, but you are in no way "attached" to the results of your conversation. The Diamonds are great at that as well, aren't they? If someone isn't interested, they don't dwell on it, and they certainly don't take it personally. They just sort of move on down the road and get back to work. They are experts at saying "N-E-X-T!"

As far as I can tell, there are only two ways to develop true posture. One way is to have such faith in yourself as an unstoppable business-builder combined with a belief that G-d is ultimately calling the shots anyway, that you work with the realization that as long as you control your activity, G-d will control the results. Easy to have true posture with that attitude.

The other way is to continually develop and have such a huge and ever-growing list of names (prospects) that you know you can never possibly run out of prospects. That will also provide you with

7

true posture.

Of course, the ideal is to have both of the above!

Let's begin talking about the second way right now. I'll leave the first way up to you and your mentors.

Know You, Like You, Trust You

Let's begin with the "Golden Rule" of Business Networking: *"All things being equal, people will do business with, and refer business to, those people they know, like and trust."*

Think about it: isn't that how you are, or were, as a consumer? Before you joined this business where you can now purchase practically *everything* you need online, isn't it true that when you considered buying a car, furniture, clothes, or anything else, if the price, service, and all other determining factors were equal (or even close to equal), you bought from - and referred to - those salespeople you felt best about? You felt as though you had a relationship with them (you *knew* them). You felt good about them (you *liked* them). And you felt as though they had your best interest in mind (you *trusted* them).

And you probably referred others to them as well, with pleasure, didn't you?

Well, it's the same here, whether we're talking about your customers, or those whom you desire to have as part of your team. Of course, for the purpose of this booklet, we're talking about building an organization, and will proceed with that in mind.

Your job is to now take on the mindset of developing relationships with people, and cultivating these relationships to the point where the new people you meet, on a daily basis, *feel good about you.* They feel so good about you that they feel as though they know you, they like you, and they trust you (and for good reason - you are the type of person who deserves those feelings toward you in another person). They want to see you succeed, they want to help you find new business, possibly they want to be a part of your business; they definitely want to be a part of your life.

And we'll talk about how to bring about those feelings in a quick and timely manner. More importantly, we'll discuss specifically how to accomplish this with comfort, in a way that makes the process of prospecting fun. That's right. . . fun! No more stomach tension because you need to go out doing something you don't want to do. No more defensiveness as you approach someone who doesn't want to be approached, to talk about something they don't want to hear about. This process will make prospecting downright fun!

The Law of 250

Joe Girard was a car salesperson based in Detroit Michigan. "So what?" you might ask, "what does that have to do with me?" Well, the car sales part maybe nothing. But the wisdom he imparts, much. You see, Joe Girard, for 14 years in a row, was listed in the *Guiness Book of World Records* as the most successful car salesperson in the world in terms of numbers sold. You've learned through the success system you plug into through your line of mentorship that wisdom in one area of life typically applies across the board, and can be applied to your business as well, correct? Well, you and I probably both believe that anyone who has been that successful for such a consistently long time, *probably* has some wisdom to impart to us that we can successfully employ. So, what is that wisdom?

In his bestselling book *How to Sell Anything to Anybody* (no, I don't like the title either, but the book itself is excellent), Joe explains what he calls *Girard's Law of 250*. His Law of 250 simply says that each of us has a personal sphere of influence (those we know *naturally*, i.e., close family, distant relatives, close friends, acquaintances, those we went to school with, work with, our plumber, tailor, barber/hairstylist, our accountant, lawyer, etc.) of about 250 people. According to Girard, that's how many people will attend

9

our wedding. . . and our funeral!

Even if his numbers for those two major events seem somewhat high, the 250 figure still works out. For instance, if you were to take a pencil and paper and write down everybody you know (and I mean *everybody*!) in accordance with the memory joggers information you received when you first joined the business, you would have a list of about 250 people. Back to this in a moment.

Please understand that when you register a new IBO and they write down only three names ("that's everyone I know" - even though they have five siblings), that isn't truly their entire sphere of influence. What they are really communicating to you is that based on their lack of knowledge about the business and lack of confidence in themselves at this time, that's all the names they are willing to *risk* sharing with you right now. That's okay, as long as you understand that. Then you are in a position to assure them that even though you are going to help them come up with 250 names right now, that you and they will only begin contacting those people once they are emotionally ready to do so.

Okay, now let's address that 250 person center of influence that everyone has. What's not so important is that *you* know 250 people. What is key is the fact that every new person you meet *also* knows 250 people. Do you see where we are going with this?

That's right, every time you meet one new person, and are able to establish and cultivate a relationship with that person, and develop that relationship to the point that that person feels as though he knows you, likes you, and trusts you - to the point that that person wants to see you succeed, wants to help you find new business, wants to possibly be a part of your business, and definitely wants to be a part of your life. . . well, let's put it this way:

** *Every time you accomplish the above successfully with one new person, you have just increased your personal sphere of influence (i.e., your inventory - your names list) by a potential 250 people*

10

EVERY SINGLE TIME! Do this with just one new person a day (or even more) and in practically no time at all, you will have developed an absolutely enormous, humongus, personal sphere of influence! **

How to Find Them, Meet Them, and Win Them Over

With that in mind, the only question left is how to do it. How to put yourself in a position, and have the personal knowledge, that allows you to add people to your names list - your inventory - on a continual basis, every day, 250 people at a time.

First we must ask, "where can we find good prospects?" The answer is "practically everywhere." But I think you already know that. So the next question is, "where can we find them in a setting that lends itself to approaching them in a very laid-back, non-threatening manner (and this is important. . . non-threatening to them, and to you!). Only then is there an opportunity to meet them, and begin the process of establishing a mutually beneficial, win/win relationship.

In the next chapter, you'll learn how to accomplish this, and build your inventory to an enormous level.

Chapter 2
The Process
(10 Steps to Cultivating Endless Prospects)

There's a good reason why the situations/places/events in which you meet quality potential prospects must be conducive to your approaching them. A reason why *both* you and the other person need to feel non-threatened, and even *good* about the process. Of course, it's pretty obvious why the *prospect* must feel this way.

The reason why it is so vitally important for *you* to feel this way is that you need to see the prospecting process as being fun. And it can be. But it's only fun when the nervousness (sick, nauseous feeling in the gut) typically associated with prospecting is no longer there. And this only happens when the situation for meeting someone you wish to prospect allows for a natural feeling of comfort. Don't worry - those situations abound! It will never again be a problem for you.

Places and Faces

So where in particular do these positive prospecting situations occur? Let's list just a few places. One would be a social/business event such as a monthly Chamber of Commerce "Business After Hours" event. Although these gatherings are typically worthless for most people - and you may have experienced that same result - they can be pure, solid gold (or should I say "Diamonds") for you. It's only a matter of approaching these events, and working them, the correct way.

Another great place to prospect is a purely social gathering, such as a party. And the more people you *don't* know, the merrier. Don't get nervous here; the prospecting process will be a breeze! I'm just wanting to help you find situations in which there are people you don't know, because those are the new people to add to your growing *inventory*.

Still another wonderful place to meet quality prospects is at local charity events. Why? Because (besides the fact that just by virtue of your being there means you are supporting a charity) charity events attract "successful givers," which are the very type of people who go Diamond! Actually, there are generally two types of people who attend charity events: those who already are successful (those are the type who *get* this business the quickest, right?), and those who are on their way to being successful. I'm sure you're willing to help both types accomplish their goals, aren't you?

The following is an awesome place to meet prospects of high quality: the super bookstore/coffee shop combination. Perfect setting. Why? Because, typically, readers are potential leaders (of course, you already know that "leaders are readers"), and many of them will begin to read a book while enjoying a delicious, relaxing cup of cappuccino. Now, if you're thinking, *"But Bob, approaching a stranger who is reading and drinking a cup of coffee is exactly what I **don't** want to do,"* don't worry. We are not near that point yet. When it's time, it'll be a piece of cake.

Plenty of other opportunities to meet great new people on a daily business will take place as well. As you become more comfortable with the prospecting process and discover how fun it truly is, your antennae will go up and situations you never recognized before (possibly because you didn't want to) will regularly appear in your life. Ball games, PTA meetings, the health club, you name it. Again, these *situations* are not new; only the way you will *see* them and *handle* them.

Begin the Process

Let's begin by pretending you are in, what would be to many people, the worst situation for prospecting you could possibly be in. You've just joined your local Chamber of Commerce and they are having a big "Business After Hours" event (or pretend it's any event with well over 100 people attending). At this point, you know *absolutely nobody* there. Bad or good? Good. . . very good!

"But, Bob, you don't understand. I'm not like my upline Sapphire, Emerald and Diamond. I mean, I'm not smooth. I can't just walk into a place where I don't know anyone and start talking to people."

Good, then you are like I am. Because nothing would scare me more than to think that I have to approach a bunch of strangers and begin talking to them about my business.

So let's back up a moment and, before we meet anyone, systemize this process.

Step Number One: Adjust your attitude to the understanding that the reason you are attending this event is to work. To build your names list. To increase your inventory. That doesn't mean you won't have fun. In fact, this type of prospecting is some of the most fun you will ever have. But you are there to work.

Step Number Two: Prepare to "work the room." How? Simply recognize the "lay of the land," so to speak. Where are the people standing and/or sitting? Where is the hors d'oeuvres table, the refreshments table? Where are the restrooms? Notice the people gathered in groups of four, five or six people who are conversing and relating to each other. Take a walk around the room and experience its feel.

Step Number Three: Locate - don't approach, just locate - several people in the room defined as "centers of influence." What do I mean by that term? Remember we spoke earlier about spheres of influence - the people you know? Well, centers of influence are those people who, themselves, already have a very large, powerful, even prestigious sphere of influence. They've been around for a while now and know a lot of people. And those people are comfortable with them. They know them, like them and trust them. These centers of influence are the people you want to make a point of meeting at this event. Can you imagine making a personal connection with two or three of *them*? Connections of the "Know *you*, like *you*, and trust *you*" variety. Wow, talk about access to lots and lots of other quality people, each with his or her own 250 person sphere of influence.

But how do you know who these centers of influence are if you don't know any of the people at the event? My good friend and prospecting mentor Rick Hill taught me a wonderful method to quickly and efficiently determine this. Just casually notice the interactions of the small groups and you'll quickly notice that one person in each group is sort of the unofficial group leader. This is the person around whom the conversation sort of revolves. In other words, when they laugh, the rest of the group laughs. When they give a disgusted look at something someone says, all others do the same. Nine times out of ten, this person is a center of influence, and well worth getting to know one-on-one. With this in mind, let's move on to. . .

Step Number Four: Meet one of these centers of influence one-on-one.

But how do you do that if they are involved in a group discussion? After all, besides the fact that breaking into someone else's (who you don't yet know) conversation is somewhat rude and will generally not accomplish what you want - good feelings toward you in the other person - it is also very awkward and scary. So again, please don't put that kind of pressure on yourself. It is totally unnecessary.

So what should you do? Just wait patiently for one of the several centers of influence you've picked out of the crowd to leave their present group. Sooner or later, one of them will. Why? For a variety of reasons. Possibly to get something to eat or drink. Use the restroom, move on to another group, meet new people with whom to network for their own business, and who knows why else. But eventually, they will move on. When that happens, be ready.

For example, let's say one of them, a young 30-something gentle-

16

man walks toward the hors d'oeuvres table. Well, head on over there as well. Stay calm, and have a warm, genuine smile on your face. Gently make eye contact with him. When he sees you, just smile and say "hello." Most likely, he'll do the same. If he doesn't, then that's fine as well. Maybe he's got something else on his mind. The timing might not be right at this point to meet him. Possibly he's just an unfriendly lout. Who knows; who cares? Just say to yourself "NEXT" and wait for another center of influence to leave *their* group.

Now let me share something with you. The chances are greater than 99 out of 100 that this person will in fact smile right back at you and say "hello." When he does, just extend your hand (or not, if he has food in one hand and a drink in the other) and introduce yourself. He will do the same. Now just ask him what line of work he is in. He'll gladly tell you, and ask you the same. Briefly mention your "J.O.B." (what you do for a livelihood until you're ready to retire and do this full-time), or respond along the lines of "I'm a business development consultant." But please keep this in mind, as this is *key*: here is where you. . . DON'T TALK ABOUT YOUR BUSINESS!!!!! Now is not the time!

Your Initial Conversation

The *only* thing you are going to talk about right now is him. Understand that he doesn't care about you and your business. He doesn't care about me and my business. *He cares about himself and his business.*

Step Number Five: Begin building rapport. This is accomplished by letting him do practically all of the talking. And you do practically all of the listening. Powerful for two reasons: one is that it is totally stress-free to you (there's no pressure on you to be witty, quick, clever, etc); two is that it's very effective for developing good feelings in him toward you. Hey, isn't it true that the people we find most *interesting* are the people who seem most *interested in us*? Sure. After all, how many times have you been in a conversation

17

with someone who let you do practically all of the talking, and then afterward said to yourself, *"Wow, what a fascinating conversationalist that person was!"* And you felt really good about them. It's happened to me, *and I know this system*!!

Step Number Six: Ask several open ended, *feel-good* questions. Open-ended questions are simply questions that cannot be answered by way of yes or no, but elicit a longer response. Open-ended questions usually (but not always) begin with "What, when, where, why, and how."

The most important part to this step however, is the *feel-good* part. *Feel-good* questions are the key. First, let's define our terms. What is a *feel-good* question? A *feel-good* question is a question that, by its very nature, results in your prospect *feeling good* about himself, about your conversation, and - most importantly - *about you*! This part of the prospecting process is the key to unlocking the door to the relationship. And the nicest part about it is that you can sort of sit back and let your prospect be the star.

Asking questions designed to make your prospect feel good about himself sort of flies in the face of some of the more traditional methods of prospecting. How many times have we heard, "Find that person's pain?" "Get them to admit they are in a rut." Of course, there is a time to do this, but this is definitely not the time. They don't know you well enough. The "know you, like you, trust you" relationship has not yet been established.

Instead of finding their pain, find their joy. Again, help him to feel good about himself. Keep in mind that everybody wears an invisible sign around his or her neck that says, "Please, make me feel important. Please make me feel good about myself." People gravitate to those who make them feel better when in their presence than when not. Isn't that how you feel around your leaders? One of my favorite Talmudic expressions is, "Who is honored? One who honors others." Honor your prospect (and everyone else in your life) by making them feel good about themselves.

So what are some of these *"Feel-good"* type questions?

I have five open-ended, feel good questions I'd like to share with you. Please understand, however, that you won't ever have time to ask all of them. You'll only have time to ask a couple of them. And the first two are probably the best. Asking only these two questions will make a significant difference in your effectiveness with your prospects. Nonetheless, let's review all five so you'll have each of them at your disposal for whenever you feel you might need them.

The Actual Questions

OEFG (Open-Ended, Feel-Good) Question Number One: "How did you get started in the 'widget' business?" I call this the "Movie-of-the-Week" question because most people love the opportunity to "tell their story" to someone. This, in a world where most people don't care enough to want to know their story. Be sure and actively listen, and be interested in what they are saying.

OEFG Question Number Two: "What do you enjoy most about what you do?" Again, you are giving them something very positive to associate with you and your conversation. It's a positive question which elicits a positive response, and good feelings. This is much better then asking the alternative question, "So, tell me about the awful job you have. . . as well as this wretched excuse for a life you live," (Only kidding, but you get the point.)

OEFG Question Number Three: "What separates your company from the competition?" I call this the *permission-to-brag* question. All our lives we're taught not to brag about ourselves and our accomplishments, yet you've just given this person carte blanche to let it all hang out.

OEFG Question Number Four: "What advice would you give someone just starting out in your line of work?" This is my *mentor* question. Don't we all like to feel like a mentor - to feel as though our answer really matters to someone? Provide your prospect an opportunity to feel like a mentor by asking this question.

OEFG Question Number Five: "What's the strangest (or funniest) incident you've ever experienced in your business? This is my *war stories* question. Bring up the good times with this one, or those moments that, even if they weren't too funny at the time, sure are in retrospect. People enjoy telling their war stories, and this question provides him or her the opportunity to do so.

OEFG "Alternative" Question: "What do you forecast as the coming trends in your industry?" This question works very well with the types who really want to share with you their knowledge of their industry. A "Cliff Claven" type (remember him from the show *Cheers*?) will love you as soon as you ask him this question.

The One "Key" Question That Will Set You Apart From Everyone Else Your Prospect Has Ever Met Before

Yes, I realize that's a very strong statement, but it's really true. Not only have I noticed it in my own life when asking people this question, but the strongest letters I receive from those who read my books, listen to my tapes, or attend my live programs have to do with this question, and the accompanying results. It really works, and you'll see why. First, know that this question is only to be asked once the initial rapport has been established. Here it is:

"How can I know if someone I'm talking to would be a good prospect for you?"

What have you done by asking that question? The answer is twofold. First, you've continued to separate yourself from the "average" person and affirmed to your prospect that you are interested in him, as opposed to just you. Most people are "I" oriented, thinking only of themselves, and it is quite obvious to the prospect. You, on the other hand, are being "You" oriented, thinking of your prospect and his needs. That is very appreciated.

Secondly, you have just given your prospect an opportunity to *actu-*

ally tell you how to help them find new business! Imagine that. No one has ever done that for him before. Most likely, his own loved ones have never done that before. But you have. And he'll have an answer for you. Most likely, an answer you would never expect to hear.

For instance, let's pretend that your prospect's name is Gary. Gary sells copying machines locally for one of the major copying machine manufacturers. He knows ways to spot a good prospect for his product that most of us are not aware of. Thus, when you ask, "Gary, how can I know if someone I'm talking to would be a good prospect for you?" Gary, after thinking a quick moment, responds, "Well, if you ever happen to be walking in an office and you notice a copying machine. . . and next to that copying machine is a wastepaper basket which is filled to the very rim with crumpled up pieces of paper, that's a really good sign that that copying machine has not been working well lately. . . and that would be an excellent prospect for me!

So Gary has just told you how to help him, how to network for him. And, more than anything, he appreciates the very fact that you asked. He is very quickly developing very positive feelings towards you. He knows that you are, in fact, a person well worth developing a relationship with.

Conclude and Move On

Step Number Seven: End your conversation with Gary. It's time for you to meet another center of influence, and begin another potentially great mutually beneficial relationship. Before leaving Gary, however, make sure you ask him for his business card. Only offer yours after he asks for it, and realize that your card will probably be thrown out after he gets home (along with the dozens of others he received at this event). Even if your business card isn't thrown out, it will at best be relegated to his Rolodex®. That's okay; that's just the way it is. What's important is that you received *his* business card. More on that in the next chapter.

Step Number Eight: Introduce yourself to your next prospect. Maybe another of the several centers of influence you noticed earlier. Or even someone else who happens to be where you are standing. Naturally, you don't want to limit yourself to just talking to certain people. After all, you never know if today's non-center of influence is tomorrow's mover-and-shaker. Or, if the person who doesn't seem particularly powerful is simply a very humble, ultra-successful person. The technique for picking out centers of influence is simply a guide to help you. Don't feel as though you need to limit yourself regarding who you talk to. And one more thing: if you see a person who looks genuinely shy and bashful and as though they could use a friendly person to speak to, go out of your way to meet them. It's just a nice thing to do. And, interestingly enough, it'll never come back to *haunt* you. Usually, just the opposite.

So, what do you do when meeting your next prospect? Well. . . nothing any different than you did with your *last* prospect. You smile, introduce yourself, and invest 99.9 percent of the conversation asking her about herself and her business. You do this via open-ended, *feel-good* questions. And then you ask her the one *key* question, "How can I know if someone I'm talking to would be a good prospect for you?" Then you'll get her card, and move along to the next person. Pretty simple, right? Just remember to have fun with this, and not put any undue pressure on yourself. You don't need to be perfect. Just keep doing this, and build on your small successes. You'll be amazed by your results, almost immediately!

By the way, the process of meeting a person, and the questions you ask, work regardless of whether it takes place at an organized event such as the one we are now imagining, or meeting in a one-on-one situation anywhere else. Later, we'll talk about how to meet people in various "non-organized event" situations. And if that was the case, there wouldn't be anything left for you to do regarding your initial conversation. Since we are at an actual event, however, you can still add to the impressions you have made thus far.

Continue to Make a Great Impression

Step Number Nine: Remember your prospect's name. It's 45 minutes later. You've met three, four or five good prospects, and are now standing by the hors d'oeuvres table, having a quick, enjoyable bite. And Gary, the copy machine salesperson you met earlier, walks over to also grab a snack. As you spot him, call him by name. "Hey Gary, good to see you again!"

He'll most likely be amazed and delighted because, by this time, he has probably forgotton *your* name. Nothing personal, and since we've all done that, it doesn't surprise us. But in remembering *his* name, you'll have again made a huge impact on him (There are good, inexpensive books you can purchase on how to remember names, but the key in this case is that you haven't tried to focus on *everyone*; just a few people. Every so often, throughout the event, glance at the people you've met to remind yourself of their names).

Key point right here: reintroduce yourself to him by name, so that he doesn't feel defensive and/or embarrassed by the fact that he didn't remember your name. So IBO Steve Johnson might say, "Hi Gary, Steve Johnson. We met a bit earlier, nice to see you again. Great food, isn't it?" Now you've totally taken the pressure off of Gary, who might even tell you that he remembered your name. Regardless of whether he did or not, you played it right by taking him "off the hook" and allowing him to feel good about himself.

Step Number Ten: Introduce those you've met to each other. I call this "creative matchmaking," yet it has nothing to do with romance. It has more to do with setting people up to do business with each other, which will cause both to feel even better about you than they already do.

Let's pretend that while you are talking to Gary, Ann Jones, whom you met earlier, walks by. She sells telephone equipment to small businesses looking to expand their telecommunications abilities. Introduce her and Gary to each other first by name, and then by profession. Tell each what the other one does for work. Now, do the ultimate in edification (taught so well by the your leaders) by explaining to each how to know who would be a good prospect for the other. Wow! You can bet that no one has ever done that for them before. You have honored them by remembering their names, their professions, and even how to know how to find good prospects for them.

Now you're on a roll! You are positioning yourself as a true center of influence, and people will respond to what you project. All this time you are just beginning to give them a hint of the fact that you're an *ace*, a person they definitely want to get to know.

Now you can even politely excuse yourself from the conversation and leave the two of them talking to each other. They will talk about the one common element in their lives up to this point. . . YOU! And how impressed they are with you. And they still don't have a clue as to what you do. That's fine. When you are ready to approach them, they'll be much more interested in agreeing to meet with you.

Now we are ready for perhaps the most misunderstood yet most fun part of the process: the follow up. And we'll look at that in detail in the next chapter.

Chapter 3
The Follow-Up
(Gently and Effectively)

Whether you met your prospect and began your "know you, like you, trust you" relationship through a chance meeting, a casual conversation (which we'll get to in the next chapter) or at a formal event such as the one described in the previous chapter, the stage is now set for you to progress to the follow-up portion of our prospecting system.

Many people are intimidated by follow-up. They imagine endless hours of unpleasantries such as data-base management, phone calls, and pestering behavior that are sure to turn off their prospects. Let's not do that.

We're going to pursue a follow-up strategy that is simple, easy, unthreatening - again, to you, and to your prospect! - and very effective.

Incidentally, if you truly want to at this point, you certainly *could* call this person and invite them to look at the business. After the way you handled yourself at your first introduction, they may very well welcome you to show them your idea. And there is a time in the future when you will do this quite often because your names list will be so big, you'll just want to hurry and get people off your list as soon as possible.

You could call Gary the next day and reintroduce yourself. He'll remember you. Why wouldn't he - you made him feel great about himself. You could then discuss with him what's happening with the Internet these days in terms of making money and income diversification, find out if he'd be interested in knowing how you are doing this for yourself, and - who knows - you might set an appointment. But the chances of him agreeing to this are not nearly as good as they will be after you have gone through a couple of the follow-up methods we're about to discuss. So, unless your list is already huge, I suggest holding off on the invite for just a bit longer.

Another Great *First* Impression

Step Number One: Send a personalized "thank you" note. Sure, we've all been taught to do that, but very few actually do it. People don't realize that in failing to follow through on this one step, they are missing out on a wonderful opportunity to niche themselves into the "feel-good" part of that person's mind. The set-up of this personalized notecard is as follows:

BURG COMMUNICATIONS, INC.

www.burg.com

BOB BURG
P.O. BOX 7002
JUPITER, FL 33468-7002
561-575-2114 • 1-800-726-3667
FAX: 561-575-2304
e-mail: BBurg@aol.com

Author: *ENDLESS REFERRALS: Network Your Everyday Contacts Into Sales* (McGraw-Hill)
WINNING WITHOUT INTIMIDATION: How To Master the Art of Positive Persuasion (Samark)

Actual size is 8-1/2 x 3 inches. Notice there is lots of space in which to write your note.

When sending this note, you'll be remembered positively for two main reasons: One is that you are probably the only one who has ever sent him this type of thank you note (or possibly *any* thank you note). The second reason is that your prospect will *see* who sent the note. Very important! More on that in a moment.

Regarding the description of your profession on your notecard, this is a touchy issue that can be handled in either of two ways. Since what is important is that your prospect feels good about *you* before you invite him to explore your business, you might want to highlight your J.O.B. on the notecard. Remember, it's only when *you* feel the time is appropriate for him to know about the business that he needs that information. On the other hand, you can use the name of your IBO company, and a description across the bottom of the notecard saying, "Helping people profit from Internet Commerce." It says a little, but not much, and it doesn't broadcast BUSINESS OPPORTUNITY, which can be a turnoff to some people. Choose which option works best for you. But - and this is a key point - before taking this to your printer, counsel with your upline regarding their advice on this issue.

The note you write to your new prospect should be brief, simple, non-pushy, and written in blue ink. Research indicates blue ink is more effective both in business and personally. The note should say something like, *"Hi Gary, Thank you. It was a pleasure meeting you. If I can ever refer business your way, I certainly will."* Then simply sign your name.

Insert your notecard into a standard #10 envelope and handwrite your prospect's name and address in blue ink, hand-stamp the envelope (no metered mail here; commemorative stamps are best) and send. The fact that the envelope is handwritten and hand stamped practically ensures the envelope will be opened and your letter read, as opposed to falling the way of junk mail.

The Impression You've Made

Let's look at what you've done. First, you have again shown that you have a lot of class and are conscientious (building both your prospect's faith and trust in you). You've shown you are a person worthy of doing business with or referring to. In other words, a person worthy of his getting to know.

What you didn't do was come on strong and try to *hard sell*, as do so many others. You simply thanked him for his time (we all like to be thanked, don't we?) and for the opportunity to have met. You also reaffirmed that you have *his* best interests in mind, with the promise to make an effort to send business his way.

Why Is The Picture So Important?
Because We Think in Pictures

Often, people will say, "Bob, I understand the reason for sending the note, but is it really important to include my picture?" The answer is yes because, as human beings, we think in pictures; thus we remember in pictures. To prove this principle to yourself, simply try *not* to picture. . . *a purple elephant.* What comes to your mind? Of course, a purple elephant. Can't be avoided. And, if by chance you pictured a gray elephant, a blue elephant, or even a pink-polka-dotted elephant, it doesn't matter. You still pictured an elephant. My suggestion is to embrace this law of life, and use it to your advantage. Make sure your prospect has the opportunity to remember exactly who you are and is able to picture what you look like.

Know in advance that sending this notecard will not normally elicit a telephone call from this person, nor any type of instant gratification. But it raises the odds significantly that when you do decide to call him to set an appointment, he will be agreeable to meeting with you. At this point, if you choose, you can call him and invite him to look at the business in much the same way mentioned at the beginning of this chapter. And, soon you will want to do that. However, if you'll take the next couple of steps first, you'll increase your odds of setting an appointment even more dramatically.

Keep Them in Your Thoughts

Step Number Two: Send any articles, newspaper or magazine clippings, or other pieces of information relating to your networking prospects personally or to their business. If you learn of something that might be helpful to them, send it on your personalized notecard.

For example, Gary, who sells copying machines, is an avid antique collector. You notice an article in your local newspaper about an antique shop going out of business that is making some extremely valuable collectibles available at very undervalued prices. Clip out the article, paper clip it to your personalized notecard, and write a brief note along the lines of, *"Hi Gary, I remember you saying how much you enjoy antiques. Thought you might find this interesting."* Then send it right out to him. Do you think he'll be impressed by your remembering him like that? You bet he will be!

Maybe you read about something that could help out Ann Jones. Remember her from the previous chapter? She sells telephone equipment to small businesses who are looking to expand their telecommunications abilities. Possibly you catch a tiny notice about a new office complex being built that will house small businesses. Perfect prospects for her! You might even do some reconnaissance work and find out who is handling the leasing. Just send a note that says, *"Hi Ann, came across the following item and thought it could be of value to you. Found out the building owners name is Ms. Garrett. Her number is xxx-xxxx. Best of success, and great prospecting!"* Then sign your name, enclose in envelope, stamp, and send. Pretty simple, right? And do you think Ann might really appreciate your thought and effort? I bet she will. And, when you decide to call her because you'd like to run a business idea by her, do you think she'll be receptive? You can bet on that one as well!

Step Number Three: Whenever you learn of a person having a particular want or need for a product or service, ask yourself, "Who do I know within my new network of prospects that can fulfill those wants or needs?" This is probably the simplest and easiest of all the follow-up steps. It is nothing more than the mindset of continual contribution to others. It's also what will make you most memorable to them, and position you as a true *center of influence* within your community.

Soon you'll become that person everyone knows (not to mention *likes and trusts*). Before you know it, you are the person that others call because they've heard that you know the answers; that you are the appropriate person who can help them. This might be for a particular product or service, but it also might be for something less direct. Possibly a mother or father wants to find their son or daughter a summer job at the town factory, and they don't know who to contact. They've heard that if anyone would know, you would. And you know what; the fact is that even if you don't know, you know someone who would know. This is a result of the brilliant job you have done networking your way to becoming a center of influence. And you are beginning to find that people are very receptive to meeting with you because of the positive reputation you have developed.

Now is the Time

Step Number Four: Now call and invite those prospects you wish to do business with. At this point, your list is growing so big and so fast that now is the time to make your calls. When you call, they know who you are. Inviting them is simply a matter of asking the right questions. And different prospects will be asked in different ways. Some you will want to meet with at their home and have an opportunity to plug in your CD. Others would be best to first have a brief meeting with at a coffee shop and leave them with your website information. Others you'll be able to invite straight to an open meeting. The choice is yours.

Phrasing the questions can also be different depending upon both the individual you are speaking with, and the methods for inviting prospects taught by your line of mentorship.

Diamonds Chuck and Colleen Goetschel first ask their prospect if they're familiar with "the incredible amount of money being made via the Internet." When the person responds positively (and they will, since that is now an accepted fact), their next question is: "If I knew of a way for you to make a substantial amount of money through e-commerce (or through the Internet), would you want to know about it?" Depending upon the person they are asking, Chuck

30

and Colleen might ask the question a bit differently. If they are talking to someone they know already has a lot of money, they may phrase the benefit in terms of "income diversification" or "getting more time back into your life."

If the person is interested, great, set up the "visit." If they are not interested at this time, you can then ask if they would be open to the idea of referring you to others who might be looking. If they enthusiastically respond that they would be open to that idea, then set a time you can get together to show him what you are doing. "Gary, I know you're the type who, before referring anyone, needs to know what it is you are referring them to." He'll most likely agree with that. Then, in order to show him what he'll be referring, you'll need to show him the plan.

Repeat this pattern with those on the list with whom you decide to cultivate a relationship, and before long, you'll be exposing your awesome business to as many people as you'd like.

You might be asking, "This process obviously works, but is there any way to find and prospect people, and 'get to the point,' even more quickly?"

Absolutely there is. And we'll discuss that in the next chapter.

Chapter 4
"Quick" Prospecting
(Lots and Lots of Prospects)

Until this point, the entire purpose of this booklet has been to help an IBO who feels at a loss for finding new prospects (and who is intimidated by the prospecting process) to be able to add continually to his or her list, and more importantly, to do so in a way that is not at all intimidating, either to the IBO or to the prospect. In other words, a method that, over a relatively short period of time, could gently and effectively expand your inventory (your list of quality names) by 250 people every single time, and on a daily basis.

Now that you are there, you will want to quicken the process a bit. In fact, you'll have such a huge list that your main goal will seem to be getting people off your list as fast as you're putting them on. That mindset makes prospecting very, very fun. And very, very comfortable.

Why? Well, remember earlier we talked about and defined *posture*? True posture is when you care, but not that much. In other words, you've got so many names on your list and people to talk to, that if someone isn't interested, you are pretty much "outta there" (in your own mind). Before they complete the word "no," you're on to the next person. What a great feeling!

With that in mind, let's go to some great places for meeting lots of quality people. Our goal in this chapter is to quickly establish relationships, ask a couple of qualifying questions, and then decide whether to bring the business up right now, or to simply get their business card and call them to set up a visit. (Remember, you can always opt to go through the follow-up process described in the last chapter if you feel more comfortable doing that).

33

Cappuccino Anyone?

An excellent place to do this is one of the super-bookstores (the ones that have a separate section for people to read while drinking coffee), or even an upscale coffee shop such as Starbuck's. Both of these venues tend to have a large number of upscale, ambitious, quality people frequenting their establishments. These are the people to keep your eye on.

Step Number One: Relax at one of the tables with a cup of coffee, cappuccino, or whatever else suits your fancy, and take out a book to read. Enjoy yourself, and the experience, knowing that there is absolutely no pressure for you to meet anyone special. When it's ready to happen, it will happen.

Step Number Two: Notice a sharp-looking person sitting down at a table near you who begins to read a book, enjoying their coffee, cappuccino, or whatever suits *their* fancy.

Step Number Three: Eventually make eye contact, smile and say hello. Say something *original* such as, "Good cappuccino, isn't it?" (Not exactly brain surgery here).

Step Number Three (addition): Any other conversation starter will do. For instance, "What are you reading?" If the person responds in a cheerful, welcoming way, you can begin to discuss their book, asking questions about it if you haven't yet read it or bringing up a certain point about it if you have. You can make comment questions such as, "aren't books great?" and then begin a very positive discussion about books.

Step Number Four: Eventually, your conversation will progress to the point where you ask what line of work they're in, and then you can ask a couple of the "open-ended, feel-good" questions. Remember the first two: "How did you get started in the widget business," and "What do you enjoy most about what you do?"

The One "Key" Statement

Step Number Five: Say the "One *Key* Statement." Whereas in the previous scenario (see Chapter 2) we asked the one key *question*, "How can I know if someone I'm talking to would be a good prospect for you?" (and, of course, you could still ask that question now if you so choose), here we're going to do something different. We're going to gently reach out to our prospect with a statement that will both qualify their interest in looking at a new business idea, and provide us with an appropriate response to their response.

This one *key* statement is:

"You must really enjoy what you do!"

Here is what you have just accomplished: First, you continued to make your prospect feel encouraged, and good about the conversation. Secondly, there is no way they feel they are being "prospected" because prospecting questions usually sound as though they are attempting to elicit dissatisfaction. Your question showed admiration and respect.

Your prospect will more than likely respond to your statement in one of two ways, and either way is fine.

Response #1: "Yes, I do love my work. It's been great. Very enjoyable and rewarding."

To this you can respond, "You know what's fascinating? If there's one thing I've learned it's that people such as yourself who are already successful, are *always* the ones who are open to {other ways of making money} or {new business ideas and strategies}.

To this, your prospect will either respond by saying:

"No, not I," or, "Yes, definitely. Why, what are you working on?" Both answers are fine. One doesn't waste your time, and the other presents you with an opportunity to introduce the business, if that's what you choose to do at this time. You might utilize Chuck and Colleen Goetschel's approach and after asking your prospect if she is familiar with what's happening on the Internet and getting an affirmative response, simply ask, "If I knew of a way for you to make a substantial amount of money (or phrase it in terms of income diversification) on the Internet, would you want to know about it?"

Or you could say, "I'm in the process of expanding an Internet-based project with some very successful people in the area. It's already showing tremendous growth potential, and we're looking for a few more leaders to work with us. Would you want to know more?" I also like what Diamond Bo Short says: "We're looking for some (pauses as though he's searching for just the right word), go-getter types." Use any words or phrases that you feel relate to your prospect, based on his or her personal situation.

Again, you'll get either a yes or a no, and you can proceed from there. This takes care of response number one. Now. . .

Response #2: "No, I hate what I do. I'm not making near the income I should be making. It's very frustrating. I'd rather be doing something else."

To this you can respond, "You know, it's interesting. Some people such as yourself are obviously very sharp and have a lot of income potential, but they're simply affiliated with the wrong vehicle." And now go into the part regarding the Internet and the business you are expanding.

Depending upon your feelings about the situation, environment, timing, whatever, you can introduce the business right there, or get their card and let them know you'll call them when you're able to in order to set up a business meeting. Your posture is excellent.

Do this with enough new people, and your inventory will expand exponentially, as will your organization.

Chapter 5
Tying It All Together
(Remember the Fundamentals)

You've got it. Just keep it simple, and don't put any undue pressure on yourself. Practice this process a few times, and before long, you're utilizing a method that can't possibly fail to put as many people in front of the business as it'll take for you to succeed.

Build on Your Small Successes

Remember to build on your small successes. If going through the entire process as described in Chapter 2 seems somewhat daunting right now, then take it one step at a time. For instance, instead of having to meet five people and engage them in full conversations complete with open-ended, feel-good questions, just say "hello" to five different people. Or to just one person. Do that and you've won.

Now begin to build on that small success. Next event you go to, say hello to seven people and introduce yourself to five people. Awesome - you're doing great!

Next event, say hello to ten people, introduce yourself to seven, and engage one person in the entire process. See what's happening??!!

Now you're ready to meet people in any type of situation and just begin lighthearted conversations in which you ask some open-ended, feel-good questions, you let them talk about themselves, and get some business cards. Then the simple, easy and effective follow-up process begins.

Utilize the *System*

The good news for you is that the correct way - a proven, duplicatable system - for building your business is already there for you. It consists of mentor-recommended books, tapes, seminars, major conventions, and voice mail. Where else can you, for such a reasonable amount of money, have access to millionaires and multi-millionaires who have successfully accomplished what you are looking to accomplish. My suggestion is not to challenge the system and try to shortcut it, but to embrace it, and let it help you accomplish your goals and dreams.

If you'll follow the prospecting method outlined in this booklet, plug totally into the *system*, and work hand-in-hand with your upline mentors, yes, you'll still have problems in your life. . . but time and money will *not* be two of them!

About the Author

As a speaker, Bob Burg shares information on two topics vital to success: "How to Cultivate a Network of Endless Prospects" and "How to Master the Art of Positive Persuasion." Bob has spoken to corporations and associations around the world, including franchises, major associations, and Fortune 500 companies.

Bob has been featured on the national ralley circuit, sharing the platform with legends such as Zig Ziglar, Radio Legend Paul Harvey, Brian Tracy, Denis Waitley, CNN's Larry King, The Today Show's Willard Scott, Mary Lou Retton, Chicken Soup for the Soul's Mark Victor Hansen, Coach Lou Holtz, the late Og Mandino, President Gerald Ford, and many others.

He is the author of *Endless Referrals: Network Your Everyday Contacts Into Sales* which has sold well over 100,000 copies; and *Winning Without Intimidation: How to Master the Art of Positive Persuasion,* which sold over 94,000 copies in just two years. Both books are available via your tool catalogue.

Bob is a staunch supporter and defender of the American Free Enterprise system.

http://www.burg.com